RESILIENCE

Introduction 4

Defining Resilience: What Is It? 6
Why Is Resilience Important? 6
Factors Of Resilience 7
Can You Build Resilience? 8
Who Can Benefit From Resilience Training? 9

Types Of Resilience For All Of Life's Hardships 11
Psychological Resilience 12
Emotional Resilience 12
Physical Resilience 13
Community Resilience 14
Using The Forms Of Resilience 15

The Components Of Resilience 18
Connection 18
Wellness 18
Healthy Thinking 19
Meaning 19
The Components Of Resilience In A Real-Life Example 20

How To Build Connections During Times Of Loss 23
Benefits Of Connection 23
Quality Vs. Quantity Connections 24
How To Build Healthy Connections 25
How To Maintain Healthy Connections 26

How To Foster Wellness During Times Of Poor Mental And Physical Health 29
How To Foster Wellness For Mental Health 30
How To Foster Wellness For Physical Health 31

How To Think Healthy Thoughts During Difficult And Uncontrollable Times 34
Recognize Thinking Traps 35
How To Think Healthy Thoughts 37

How To Find Purpose When You Feel Lost 40
Why Purpose Helps Resilience 40
Purpose And Meaning 41
How To Find Your Purpose 41

Bringing It All Together: Resilience Training 45
Resilience Training 45
Training Your Attention 46

Conclusion 50

INTRODUCTION

If you have a computer, read self-help books, or occasionally watch shows like Oprah or Dr. Phil, then you have probably heard about resilience at one point or another. Even as a child, you may have been told that you need to become more resilient, you need to grow your resilience, or that you need to encourage your friends to be resilient.

People love to tell you to be resilient, but they rarely give you advice on how to do it, leaving you with more questions than answers. What is resilience, and why does it matter? Why are doctors, counselors, and friends all the sudden talking about resilience in your life? Is it a new phenomenon, or have doctors been looking at it for a while? Better yet, how do you become resilient, and how can it help your life?

In short, resilience is your way to bounce back from adverse situations. Resilience is absolutely necessary to live a healthy, happy, and high-quality life. Without resilience, it is easy to get defeated, feel worn down by life, and eventually give up on yourself or others. Resilience, though, will help you overcome any difficult situation and allow you to live a better life, no matter how tough the situation may be.

In this book, we look at resilience and offer you key tips for building mental strength to overcome difficult situations. We begin by defining resilience, discussing the four types of resilience, and looking at the four components of resilience. Then, we offer examples and suggestions for developing these components so that you build your resilience.

We hope that you use this book to approach adverse situations with confidence an intelligence so that way you can overcome those situations and live a better life. Let's get started.

CHAPTER 1

DEFINING RESILIENCE: WHAT IS IT?

DEFINING RESILIENCE: WHAT IS IT?

In short, resilience is the ability to bounce back from life's adversities, stressful events, and emotionally-taxing situations. Resilience allows people to grow, heal, and overcome their situations instead of letting hard times get the best of them.

Without resilience, people can quickly become sad, overwhelmed, and tired of their life. In fact, having little resilience is one of the main reasons why people feel overwhelmed by their situations, get burnt out at their job, and feel as though they are living a less-than-ideal life.

With this in mind, resilience is the key to overcoming any difficult situation and living a better life. So, it is imperative to know the limits of your own resilience and learn new techniques to become more resilient in the future.

Why Is Resilience Important?

Resilience is highly important for one's quality of life. In fact, resilience is one of the highest determiners for one's enjoyment, fulfillment, and growth throughout life. For this reason, resilience is important for living the best life possible.

If you do not learn resilience, you can easily be taken down by any of life's challenges. Some of the most common adversities faced in life include the following:

- Changing careers
- Stressful work environment
- Divorce

- Death of a loved one
- Financial troubles
- Moving
- Raising children
- And more

All of these scenarios require resilience in order to bounce back stronger than before. If you are resilient, you are more likely to bounce back from these situations, even though they will still be tough when you're experiencing them.

Take divorce, for instance. If you are going through a tough divorce and are not resilient, you can easily feel as though your life is falling apart and that there is no point in love. This then will eventually cause you to feel even more upset by your situation and potentially ruin future relationships.

If you are resilient though, divorce will still be difficult, but you will learn how to cope with its hardships and learn from the experience. As a result, you may find a better relationship in the future and avoid making the same mistakes with that partner.

Factors Of Resilience

Although resilience looks different for every person, there are certain factors that most, if not all, resilient people have in common. Here are the most important factors of resilience:

- **Social Support:** Social support is one of the top determiners of resilience. Resilient people almost always have a strong support system made up of their family members, friends, and community.

- **Realistic Planning:** Resilient people are realistic in terms of their abilities, limitations, and control. This allows them to make and execute realistic plans that play up their strengths and work around their weaknesses.

- **Confident:** Confidence is an important aspect of resilient people. Resilient people know their strengths and abilities, which allows them to confront adversity with confidence.

- **Healthy Coping Mechanisms:** Having healthy coping mechanisms is a crucial aspect of resilience. Coping mechanisms allow a resilient person to problem-solve their way through adversity and overcome the hardship.

- **Strong Communication:** Resilient people have strong communication skills. This allows them to communicate when they need help achieving a goal, finding resources, or taking action.

- **Regulate Emotions:** Resilient people manage overwhelming emotions healthily and respectfully. This allows them to acknowledge the emotion without letting it overcome them.

Can You Build Resilience?

At this point, you may be thinking, "What if I am not resilient?" Luckily for you, resilience can be built. It is not a destination that people land on or a genetic predisposition that people are born with. Instead, resilience is nothing more than a journey that is built through time, hard work, and patience.

There are a number of resilient-building skills that can be learned and taught. If you think you are not resilient, you can break through your current habits to become more resilient in the future. In order to become more resilient though, you need to be self-aware of your current shortcomings and bad habits and change them so that way they are healthier and resilient-driven.

In the upcoming chapters, we look at key strategies for improving your resilience so that you can overcome all adversities in life.

Who Can Benefit From Resilience Training?

Since everyone faces adversities in life, anyone can benefit from resilience training. From the most resilient to the least resilient person, resilience training will help you become a better version of yourself so that you are better able to deal with challenges in the future.

CHAPTER 2
TYPES OF RESILIENCE FOR ALL OF LIFE'S HARDSHIPS

TYPES OF RESILIENCE FOR ALL OF LIFE'S HARDSHIPS

Interestingly, there are four types of resilience: psychological, emotional, physical, and community. Each type is useful for different situations, meaning you will use specific types of resilience to combat specific scenarios in your life. This allows you to tailor the resilience strategy for the difficult situation you are currently facing. At the same time, though, it is important to note that most adverse situations require more than one type of resilience at a time.

Let's take a look at the four types of resilience. For every resilience type, we will look at how each type affects major life problems, temporary problems, and daily problems.

- **Major Life Problems:** Major life problems are those that have a lasting impact on your life. This can include the death of a loved one, incurable illness, divorce, losing a job, or anything else that will impact your life significantly.

- **Temporary Problems:** Temporary problems are those that disrupt your daily life but do not last more than a month or so. Things such as the flu, a tough deadline at work, your child's upcoming math exam, or a tough criticism said by your significant other are all temporary problems.

- **Daily Problems:** Daily problems are those that we face every day. Everyday chores, an annoying coworker, or exercising regularly are all daily problems. Daily problems rarely have a significant impact on your life.

Psychological Resilience

Psychological resilience, or mental resilience, is when you are able to think clearly, flexibly, and creatively. In many ways, psychological resilience is your ability to problem-solve, conceptualize goals, and execute strategies. Without psychological resilience, you might not be able to effectively think through tough situations.

- **Major Life Problems:** Psychological resilience is key to bouncing back from major life changes, such as the death of a loved one, divorce, or career change. If you are not psychologically resilient, it can be difficult to interpret the pain you're feeling and strategize away to becoming happier and healthier in the future.

- **Temporary Problems**: Instances such as temporary illness, an impending deadline, or an angry client are all instances of short-term problems that require psychological resilience. Psychological resilience will allow you to overcome these challenges by interpreting the problem and coming up with effective solutions.

- **Daily Problems**: Every day, we face daily challenges that require us to be psychologically resilient. For example, whenever you are doing puzzles, trying a new hobby, or reading a book, you have to be engaged and have psychological resilience. Although daily life might not require high amounts of psychological resilience, psychological resilience will allow you to better enjoy and succeed in your daily life.

Emotional Resilience

Arguably one of the most difficult types of resilience to master is emotional resilience. Emotional resilience is your ability to accept adversities and find positive outlooks in grim circumstances. Emotional resilience is keenly connected to emotional intelligence, emotional awareness, perseverance, and optimism.

- **Major Life Problems:** Emotional resilience is an important way to handle major life problems, such as getting fired, a divorce, or a death in the family. It allows us to understand our emotions but also understand that it will get better over time. Without emotional resilience, major life problems can easily feel overwhelming and all-encompassing.

- **Temporary Problems:** Often, we find ourselves angry or upset whenever someone doesn't act the way we think they should. This creates temporary problems that require emotional resilience. Emotional resilience allows us to understand that the problem is only temporary, cope with our emotions in a healthy way, and prepare our emotions for the next time we find ourselves in a similar situation.

- **Daily Problems:** Every day, emotional resilience is used to help us imagine, dream, and create the life we want. We often reflect on our lives through writing, making art, or walking. Emotional resilience is the key to helping us understand our reflections and feelings.

Physical Resilience

Physical resilience is our body's capacity to face and accomplish physical challenges, maintain stamina, and recover whenever injured. Physical resilience can be important if you have a major life-altering injury or find yourself in a life-threatening situation.

- **Major Life Problems:** It is important to be physically resilient whenever you have a life-altering injury such as spinal surgery or a car accident. After these injuries, it will take months to recover to your original state, if at all. Your ability to keep moving, work through the pain, and get stronger is an example of physical resilience.

- **Temporary Problems:** Temporary problems that require physical resilience include things like marathons, hiking, or sports. These instances require physical resilience, but you often voluntarily put yourself in these situations. With that being said, there are also situational problems that you have no control over, such as domestic violence. In these situations, you need physical resilience in order to perform your best under short-term pressure.

- **Daily Problems:** Every day, we need to be physically resilient. From walking to getting a good night's sleep, physical resilience allows us to stay healthy and happy. Eating healthily, exercising daily, and sleeping well are all parts of physical resilience on a daily basis.

Unlike the two previous forms of resilience, physical resilience is physically painful and physically taxing. It will be easier to see the results of physical resilience, though. Additionally, emotional and psychological resilience can impact your physical resilience.

For example, suppose you are in a bad car accident and need to go through extensive physical therapy. If you are not emotionally and psychologically resilient, it will be more difficult to work through the pain and be physically resilient.

Community Resilience

The last form of resilience, community resilience, is different from the other three forms. The first three forms of resilience deal with one's ability to be resilient to different situations. Community resilience, on the other hand, deals with a community's ability to be resilient and respond to adverse situations.

Community resilience is important for instances such as natural disasters, acts of violence, or economic hardships. Examples of community resilience include Newtown, Connecticut after the Sandy Hook Elementary school shooting; New Orleans after Hurricane Katrina; and New York City after the 9/11 terrorist attacks.

Although community resilience is highly important, we will not focus on community resilience in this book. Instead, we will focus on the first three forms of resilience since they are what you have control over.

Using The Forms Of Resilience

Let's look at a stressful scenario and discuss how each form of resilience would or would not help the situation. Take, for instance, that you have lost your job and do not know where you will get your livable income.

- **Psychological Resilience:** Psychological resilience is important when you lose your job. It will allow you to both learn from your mistakes and strategize or brainstorm ideas for new job leads. In other words, it helps you think your way out of the problem.

- **Emotional Resilience:** Emotional resilience is important when you lose your job too. Losing your job can take a blow to your self-esteem, causing you to feel inadequate and incompetent. Emotional resilience allows you to interpret those feelings and see the light at the end of the tunnel. In other words, it prevents your emotions from getting the best of you.

- **Physical Resilience:** Physical resilience may help you when you lose your job. If you are finding that getting fired is extremely difficult for you emotionally and mentally, you should use your physical resilience to offset those feelings. You can go to the gym, jog, or eat healthily in order to combat those feelings of inadequacy and stress.

This situation exemplifies that you may need to use more than one, if not all, types of resilience to combat adverse situations.

CHAPTER 3

THE COMPONENTS OF RESILIENCE IN A REAL-LIFE EXAMPLE

THE COMPONENTS OF RESILIENCE

Regardless of the type of resilience, there are certain components that make up all types of resilience. These components make resilient thinking meaningful and impactful in your life. Without these components, it can be difficult to become resilient or to experience the benefits of resilience. Let's look at the four components of resilience: connection, wellness, healthy thinking, and meaning.

Connection

Connection is your ability to connect with your family members, friends, and community. It is a common misconception that resilient people do not need help from others, but this misconception is completely false. In contrast, the most resilient people have some of the strongest connections around.

The reason that connection is important for resilience is that it allows you to have a support system whenever you fail. Without having anyone to talk to or help you, you can easily feel overwhelmed by your life and have nowhere to turn to whenever you fail.

Wellness

Wellness is the active process of becoming more aware and making choices to become healthy and living a fulfilling life. Although wellness includes being physically fit and healthy, it is intimately related to emotional and mental change and growth as well. It is important to have wellness in order to live a high-quality life.

Wellness relates to your physical health, mental health, emotional health, and personal growth. Wellness matters for resilience since the point of resilience is to make you happier and healthier over time: resilience contributes to your wellness, and your wellness contributes to your resilience.

As you become more resilient, your wellness increases. At the same time, as you focus more on your wellness, your resilience is more likely to increase as well. Without wellness, you are unlikely to become resilient now or in the future.

Healthy Thinking

Healthy thinking is your ability to think realistically, flexibly, and creatively. For you to think healthily, you must be able to accurately interpret a situation, strategize how you're going to handle it, and effectively execute your strategy. More so, healthy thinking is about learning from your mistakes and incorporating them into your new plans, goals, and strategies.

Resilience depends heavily on healthy thinking. If you cannot think healthily, you will not be able to realistically interpret or effectively handle stressful situations. Instead, you will likely misinterpret the situation and think of poor ways to handle your stress or emotions.

If you think healthily, though, resilience comes much easier. The reason for this is that healthy thinking will allow you to accurately understand a situation, which will then allow you to properly respond to it.

Meaning

Meaning is the ability to connect events, ideas, and feelings into a greater purpose of life. Meaning is what allows your life, actions, and ideas to feel impactful and meaningful in the world around you. If you do not have meaning, it is easy to feel dragged down by life's adversities.

Resilience depends highly on meaning. The reason for this is that meaning gives motivation for resilience. It allows resilience to have a purpose, goal, and context.

The Components Of Resilience In A Real-Life Example

Andrea has been married to Jeremy for 20 years, but they have decided that it is time to get a divorce. In order to get through this divorce, Andrea needs resilience so that she can come back stronger than before. More specifically, her resilience strategy must incorporate connection, wellness, healthy thinking, and meaning.

- **Connection:** Now that she is single, Andrea feels lonely and isolated. To bounce back from these feelings, she needs to strengthen her connections with her family members and loved ones. She could spend extra time with her parents, go to the gym with a friend, or go to a Community Center to make new friends over shared interests or hobbies. Strengthening her connections allows her to feel loved and appreciated again.

- **Wellness**: Like most divorcees, Andrea feels insecure, stuck, and unsure. To be resilient, she needs to focus on her wellness. Wellness includes developing healthy habits, being kind to herself, or going to a counselor. Focusing on her wellness allows her to improve her life and get the most out of this phase.

- **Healthy Thinking:** Andrea is beginning to question her competence in making life decisions. She feels like she married the wrong person, wasted her youth, and failed miserably. To bounce back, she needs to think healthily about her marriage and current state. She did not make a mistake, waste her youth, or fail. Instead, she and Jeremy changed, and it is now best to separate. Thinking healthily allows her to learn from her mistakes, grow, and not wallow.

- **Meaning:** Since her marriage failed, Andrea feels disconnected from life and herself; she doesn't know who she is or what she wants. Andrea should actively try to find a way to connect meaning to her new life. Additionally, she should view the divorce itself as having meaning, such as giving her the opportunity to live her best life possible. Developing a new meaning creates importance and context for her new life.

In this example, as well as any other situation you will face in life, it is important to combine all four components at the same time. You should not just focus on one over the other. Instead, you should have a holistic perspective on your resilience-strategy that includes connection, wellness, healthy thinking, and meaning.

If you only focus on one component, you will not become as resilient as you could. For example, if you only focus on your connections, you could still harbor unhealthy thoughts about your marriage and divorce. This will result in a number of unwanted consequences on your present and future, regardless of how strong your connections are.

With this in mind, approach all of your adverse situations with the mentality of tackling them. You will tackle these situations by emphasizing your connections, wellness, thinking, and meaning.

CHAPTER 4
HOW TO BUILD CONNECTIONS DURING TIMES OF LOSS

HOW TO BUILD CONNECTIONS DURING TIMES OF LOSS

Times of loss can be some of the most difficult, challenging, and stressful times in a person's life. Whether it's losing a job, losing a spouse, or losing your health, loss requires resilience so that way you can mourn properly but bounce back for the future.

One of the best ways to bounce back from times of loss is to build your connections elsewhere. As we have previously discussed, having strong support systems is an imperative part of being resilient. If you do not have a good support system, you may have nowhere to turn to if you're lost and need help back up.

Benefits Of Connection

Once again, connections are a vital part of resilience. The reason for this is that human beings are social creatures and having good connections and relationships with other human beings results in a number of healthy benefits.

In fact, studies have shown that the absence of connection causes distress. In situations that are already stressful, lacking emotion exacerbates the distress. More so, lacking good social support leads to poor mental health, poor cardiovascular health, and other health problems.

In contrast, though, having a strong support system is good for your wellbeing and health. Here are some benefits of having valuable connections in your life:

- Improves your ability to cope

- Alleviates the effects of distress
- Promotes lifelong good mental health
- Improve self-esteem
- Lowers cardiovascular risks
- Promotes healthy lifestyle habits

Quality Vs. Quantity Connections

With that being said, it is important to distinguish quality versus quantity connections. In order to get the most benefits of your social support network, it is important to fill your network with people who are kind, supportive, and challenge you to grow. If your network is full of people who really don't care about you, it will not be supportive during your times of need.

With this in mind, it is imperative to look for connections that are valuable to both you and the other person. Obviously, there's nothing wrong with having a lot of connections. The more the merrier. However, make sure that these connections are valuable and truly care about you. Having quality connections will provide you a place to go when you need help, support, or advice.

For most people, family members are a great place to look for quality connections. Most family members, such as parents or siblings, already care about you and only want the best for you. Additionally, close friends and community members also are good options for quality connections.

How To Build Healthy Connections

If you do not have many quality connections at the moment, that is okay. You are not alone. Many people feel isolated and alone in the world. Although this is your current state, it doesn't have to be your future one. There are ways to build your connections so that way you are less isolated in the future.

Even if you already have a lot of connections, there's nothing wrong with looking for more. As social creatures, we love to be challenged by and engaged with a variety of people. So, these ideas might work for you even if you already have a large social support network.

Here are some good ideas to help you find connections for your social support network:

- **Volunteer:** One of the best ways to find connections is to volunteer at a local charity or organization that you care about. Volunteering will allow you to connect with your community, as well as meet others who share similar interests and values. Not only will volunteering get you connections, but it will also help you connect to a deeper meaning at the same time.

- **Join A Fitness Group:** Another way to find connections is to join a fitness group. Since daily exercise should already be a part of your daily schedule, it is a good idea to join a group so that way you are continuing to exercise while meeting new people. Look at gyms in your area or go to a local Community Center.

- **Take A Class:** You can also take a class at a local college or Community Center to meet new people interested in a similar topic. Not only will this class expose you to potential connections, but it will also cultivate your psychological resilience as it teaches you new hobbies and ideas.

- **Look Online:** With the modern age, one of the best ways to meet people is online. Joining Facebook groups or following inspirational people on Instagram can be a great way to connect with people with similar interests and mentalities. There are even online support groups for specific times of loss, which will allow you to connect with people who are experiencing the same feelings as you. Make sure to pick a reputable site and be cautious about arranging in-person meetings.

How To Maintain Healthy Connections

Once you have met people who you like and want to deepen your relationship with, it is important to develop and maintain the connections. Here are some ways to nurture your relationships so that way they may turn into a healthy support system in the future:

- **Stay In Touch:** Always stay in touch. Answer phone calls, return emails, and offer invitations. This lets them know that you care about them.

- **Don't Be Jealous:** Another way to develop your connections is to not be jealous whenever the other person succeeds. Show that person that you are happy for their success.

- **Listen:** Make sure to listen when the other person is talking. Though this may sound obvious, many people ruin relationships because they are too busy talking about themselves to listen to the other person.

- **Give Back:** If your friend is always available for you and listens to you, do the same for them. Give back whatever they give to you.

- **Don't Overdo It:** Make sure not to be too overeager or overwhelm your friend with messages, calls, or talks of your feelings.

If you do these things, you are more likely to find and develop your relationships. Even if some of your connections have been around for years, it is important to maintain them so that way they will be there for you in the future as well.

HOW TO FOSTER WELLNESS DURING TIMES OF POOR MENTAL AND PHYSICAL HEALTH

Mental health is an important part of living a well-lived life. Unfortunately, poor mental health floods society. In fact, it is estimated that 7.6% of persons aged 12 years and older experience depression, and there about 47,173 suicide deaths a year. With these stats in mind, it is no wonder that we are currently going through a mental health crisis.

More so, physical health is an equally important aspect of living a high-quality life. Although life expectancies are increasing over time because of advancements in medicine, many people still struggle with incurable diseases every day or are diagnosed with painful disorders that affect their daily lives.

Because of this, it is important to foster wellness during times of poor mental and physical health. Of course, wellness may not treat or cure the underlying issue, but it might alleviate symptoms or allow you to comprehend the disease better.

To help you foster wellness during these difficult times, here are some important strategies and techniques for fostering wellness. Before discussing these techniques, it is important to mention that none of these ideas are meant to replace medical advice or attention. Do not change any medications or take on new practices without consulting your doctor first.

How To Foster Wellness For Mental Health

Wellness, in terms of mental health, means actively trying to make your mental health better. If you are struggling with your mental health, it is important to be as optimistic and kind to yourself as possible. Remember that you are worthy and capable of growth, even if it feels like you are drowning.

When fostering wellness for your mental health, it is important to listen to your feelings and thoughts so that way you can do what is best for your needs. Here are some ideas for fostering wellness for mental health:

- **Start A Gratitude Journal:** A gratitude journal gives you the opportunity to focus on things that you are thankful for. Even during times of poor mental health, there is always something that you can be happy about. Focusing on one or two things you're grateful for a day will help you to look past your negative thoughts and feel more optimistic throughout the day.

- **Meditate:** Meditation is the art of trying to sharpen your focus and mind. Meditation is a great practice for improving your mental health because it allows you to acknowledge your thoughts and feelings as they come to you but gently release them as the thought finishes.

- **Say Positive Affirmations:** Affirmations have been proven to help alleviate symptoms of poor mental health and increase optimism. Say positive affirmations that are tailored to your needs and feelings morning and night. You can either say the affirmations out loud or in your head.

- **Talk To Your Connections:** Your connections are there to help you when you need a friend. Talk to a well-trusted connection when you need to talk about your thoughts and feelings.

- **Talk To A Health Care Professional:** Talking to a health care professional can be one of the best ways to foster wellness for your mental health. Doing so will give you the opportunity to talk through your feelings and gain helpful and effective strategies for coping and working past them.

Though these ideas may take a while for you to see an impact from, it is important to keep trying and to make them a habit. If you are having extreme difficulty with your mental health, make sure to talk to a health care professional.

How To Foster Wellness For Physical Health

Physical wellness has to do with your health as well as improving it, no matter your starting point. Depending on the health conditions or needs, the strategies you implement will look different from person to person.

It is important to consult a doctor about what is best for your needs. Do not push yourself unnecessarily or cause yourself any pain. Instead, focus on pushing yourself to be just a little bit better than before so that you are challenged, but not defeated.

Here are some ideas for fostering wellness for your physical health:

- **Exercise:** If able, exercise. Depending on your limitations or illnesses, exercising may be really restricted, potentially causing you to feel like you are not working out at all. Just remember to try your best and to be patient with yourself. If all you can do is walk a few steps, then walk a few steps. Then, celebrate yourself for doing it. Celebrating your accomplishment will improve your mental health and encourage you to continue working.

- **Eat Healthily:** No matter what physical illness you may be going through, you can always eat healthily. Make sure to eat healthy vegetables, fruits, and proteins. Doing so will fuel your body with proper energy that will help your body to protect and heal itself.

- **Get Your Friends Involved:** Improving your physical wellness is difficult when you don't have any support. Utilize your connections to make physical health fun and to hold you accountable.

- **Sleep:** Although it may seem obvious, make sure that you prioritize sleep. Sleep gives your body the chance to rest and heal itself. If you are having issues concerning your physical health, make sure to sleep an ample amount of time every night. Also, make sure it is quality sleep, meaning that you stay asleep throughout the night.

Once again, these ideas for fostering physical wellness are not meant to replace medical advice. Do not push yourself past limits or harm yourself in any way.

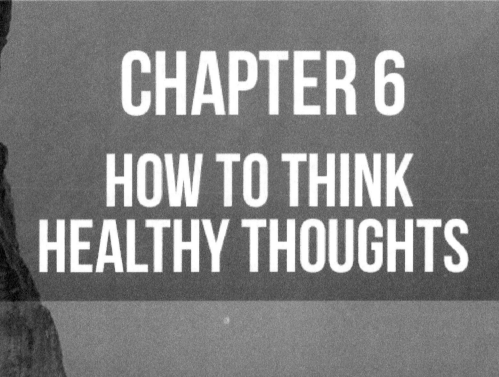

CHAPTER 6
HOW TO THINK HEALTHY THOUGHTS

HOW TO THINK HEALTHY THOUGHTS DURING DIFFICULT AND UNCONTROLLABLE TIMES

Whenever you're going through a difficult time, it can be really easy to get caught up in unhealthy thinking. These unhealthy thoughts make you feel even worse about the situation even if they do not accurately reflect the situation at all.

Unhealthy thinking can be especially difficult to avoid if the difficult time is also uncontrollable. Uncontrollable situations immediately cause humans to play out scenarios, question the past, and question our abilities. As a result, we get stuck in a cycle of unhealthy thinking that perpetuates a negative mentality and diminishes resilience.

For example, take Susan's experience with the loss of her father. Susan and her father were very close, and they had a relationship until the day he died. He died in unforeseen circumstances, specifically a car accident on the way back from a doctor's visit, preventing Susan from saying her goodbyes. As a result, Susan keeps replaying his potential last moments, asking herself why she didn't offer to take him, and dwelling on their lost time.

All these thoughts that Susan had in her head were unhealthy and were causing her to not be resilient to the situation, despite her maturity and intelligence. Susan's story is meant to show that it can be very easy to get swept away in unhealthy thinking, even if you are a completely rational and intelligent person.

Recognize Thinking Traps

One of the most important ways to think healthy is to recognize thinking traps. Thinking traps are unhealthy ways of thinking that are common whenever we feel sad, angry, anxious, depressed, or stressed. Additionally, you can fall into thinking traps just whenever you are tired or not eating well. Here are the most common thinking traps as well as examples of them:

- **Overgeneralization:** Overgeneralization is when you connect a negative situation to a constant cycle of bad things that happen. Using words like "always" or "never" is a common sign of overgeneralization.

    o **Example:** I wanted the last slice of pizza, but Hannah always took it as usual. I never get the last slice of pizza.

- **Black And White Thinking:** black and white thinking is when you see things as only being completely right or wrong, good or bad, or perfect or terrible. People who think in black and white tend to see things as a complete failure or complete success, with no middle ground.

    o **Example:** I didn't go to the gym today. My exercise plan is now a failure.

- **Labeling:** Labeling is when you only say negative things about yourself or others.

    o **Example:** I missed a question on an exam. I am stupid.

- **Mind Reading:** Mind reading is when you jump to a conclusion about what others are thinking even if you have no evidence to support it.

    - **Example:** Jeremy canceled on me. He must be going on a date with someone else.

- **Fortune Telling:** Fortune telling is when you predict something bad will happen even if there is no evidence to support it.

    - **Example:** Our relationship is going great and has progressed to the next stage, engagement, but I will say no because it will probably not work out anyways.

- **Mental Filter:** Mental filter is when you only focus on the negative parts of a situation an ignore the good.

    - **Example:** I got a raise, but I did not get the full amount that I had asked for. I must not be a good employee.

- **Emotional Reasoning:** Emotional reasoning is when you believe that your feelings reflect the situation.

    - **Example:** I am upset because I feel like Jeremy does not care about me. Therefore, Jeremy must not care about me.

- **"Should" Statements:** Should statements are when you tell yourself how you should or must act.

    - **Example:** I should be able to handle this project without getting stressed.

- **Discounting Positives:** Discounting positives is when you discount the positive things that you do or are said about you.

- **Example:** Elizabeth said that my hair looked nice, but she was just being kind.

As you can see, there are a number of thinking traps that you can fall victim to. It is important to recognize whenever you fall into a thinking trap so that way you can get out of it and practice techniques to prevent you from making the same mistake in the future.

How To Think Healthy Thoughts

If you find yourself thinking unhealthy thoughts, there are a number of ways to improve your thinking abilities, here are the most common:

1. Separate Your Thoughts From Actual Events

One of the most common reasons why people think unhealthily is that they think their thoughts are the same as the event. Consider the actual event and compare it to your interpretation of it. What actually happened? What facts would everyone agree on? How do you feel? What are your behaviors? How do other people feel? What are their behaviors?

2. Identify and Challenge Thinking Traps

Whenever you are thinking unhealthy thoughts, identify the thinking trap you're falling victim to and challenge it. For example, if you see that you are falling victim to black and white thinking, try to pose a middle ground perspective on the situation. You can challenge the thinking trap by examining the evidence, seeing if there is a double standard, or conducting an experiment.

3. Accept Your Limitations

Another common culprit for unhealthy thoughts is ignoring your limitations. There are certain things that we as humans are simply unable to do. If you find yourself in an uncontrollable situation, recognize that it is uncontrollable, and cut off any thoughts that imply you have control over the situation.

CHAPTER 7
HOW TO FIND PURPOSE WHEN YOU FEEL LOST

HOW TO FIND PURPOSE WHEN YOU FEEL LOST

If you're feeling lost, it is important to re-find your purpose. Chances are, a difficult situation, whether it be a divorce or the death of a family member, has caused you to feel separated from your life's purpose, and you feel as though your purpose has been taken from you and you don't know where you are in the world anymore. If you feel like this, it's completely understandable to feel beat down by adverse situations.

Whenever you have purpose, life tends to come easier. Work has meaning, friends are more enjoyable, and your life has context. Purpose is what makes life meaningful and worthwhile. Without purpose, though, it can be difficult to get up in the morning, let alone go to a job you hate or work on a marriage that simply isn't working.

According to Dr. Bill Damn, Director of the Stanford Center for Adolescence, purpose is "a stable and generalized intention to accomplish something meaningful to the self and consequential to the world." Dr. Damon also goes on to explain that purpose is crucial to a healthy lifestyle that is both rewarding and enjoyable.

With this in mind, it is imperative to find purpose whenever you feel lost. Without purpose, you may never feel unlost and bounce back from whatever situation you are facing.

Why Purpose Helps Resilience

Having purpose is extremely important to your resilience. Purpose gives you something to live for. In other words, it gives you a reason to want to be resilient and bounce back. Without a purpose, you may not even feel the need to be resilient or bounce back from a difficult situation.

With this in mind, resilience depends on knowing your life's purpose, even if it is fluctuating. Your life's purpose will fluctuate and change overtime. If it doesn't, you're probably not growing or pushing yourself at all. So, it is completely fine if your purpose is changing or non-definite.

Purpose And Meaning

In the chapter about the components of resilience, one of the components mentioned was meaning, where we explained that resilience is deeply connected to one's meaning in life. In this chapter, we look at how purpose can add to your life's meaning.

According to Dr. Damon's definition of purpose, purpose is a stable generalized idea of how to do something meaningful with your life. As a result, when you have a purpose, you have a dedicated meaning, and you have something to hold onto whenever you are going through adverse situations.

How To Find Your Purpose

Finding your purpose involves three things: something in the world or a problem you care about, your natural gifts, and what you love to do or your interests. Your purpose should involve all three.

Finding your purpose will take a lot of brainstorming and researching, but it will be worth it. Consider making a Venn diagram that includes the three previously mentioned factors. The center of the Venn diagram tells you ideas for your purpose.

Here are some questions to think about when trying to find your purpose:

- What did you love doing as a child?
- What do you do in your spare time?
- What is something you always wanted to do?
- What is something that excites or challenges you?
- What are you good at?
- What have other people said you are good at?
- Do you have any training or specific skills?
- What is the topic you're passionate about?
- What is something you are interested in?
- What do you daydream about?
- If you could change one thing in the world, what would it be?
- If you could do anything with your life, what would it be?
- What do you find yourself thinking about when you should be working?
- What do you want to change about your life?

Asking yourself these sorts of questions may help you evaluate and understand the problems you care about, your natural gifts, and your interests.

Once again, it is important to remember that your purpose is not definite and never changing. In contrast, your purpose changes as you do. If you find that the purpose you settled on a year ago does not fit anymore, that is fine. Simply come up with a new purpose. There is nothing wrong with changing yourself and your purpose, and, in fact, it is normal and healthy.

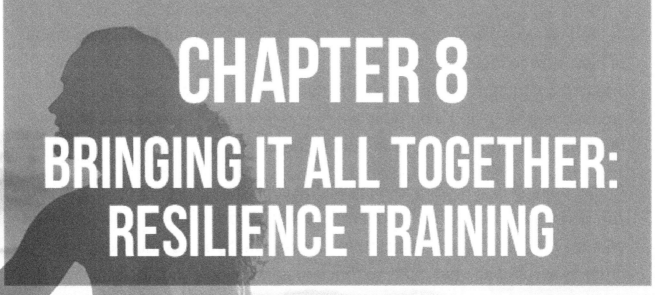
CHAPTER 8
BRINGING IT ALL TOGETHER: RESILIENCE TRAINING

BRINGING IT ALL TOGETHER: RESILIENCE TRAINING

In the last four chapters, we looked at how to build connection during times of loss, how to foster wellness during times of poor mental and physical health, how to think healthy thoughts during difficult and uncontrollable times, and how to find a purpose when you feel lost. The contents of these four chapters directly discuss the components of resilience.

At this point, it is important to bring all the components together so that you can boost your resilience and overcome any adverse situation that comes your way. In other words, it's time to discuss what you can do today in order to strengthen your mind so that you can bounce back from all of life's challenges.

Resilience Training

We call learning how to boost resilience "resilience training." Much like endurance training or weight training in the gym, resilience training will take a lot of time and effort to master, and you will always be able to get better.

Additionally, resilience training is like other training in that it is holistic. In other words, it focuses on all four components of resilience: connection, wellness, healthy thinking, and meaning. Some days you may need to emphasize one component over another, but it is important to treat each component equally.

Training Your Attention

According to the Mayo Clinic, training your attention and awareness is the most important exercise of resilience training. The reason that training your attention is so important for resilience training is that being attentive will allow you to recognize your feelings, your thoughts, and the world around you. Attention training includes becoming more intentional and purposeful in your life.

As previously stated, training your attention requires you to draw attention to your feelings and thoughts so that way you can interpret how you feel, strategize solutions, and connect meaning to the world around you. In addition to boosting resilience, training your focus also decreases stress, decreases anxiety, and boosts your quality of life.

Additionally, training your attention requires you to utilize psychological, emotional, and physical resilience even when you are undergoing a minimal amount of stress. Here is how attention training relates to the three main types of resilience:

- **Psychological Resilience:** Training your attention requires psychological resilience because it requires you to focus your mind so that way it does not wander aimlessly. As you train your attention, you also train your psychological resilience.

- **Emotional Resilience:** A key aspect of training your attention is either being able to step aside from your emotions when they are unhealthy or acknowledging them when they are healthy. In other words, it forces you to discern between necessary and healthy thoughts and emotions and unnecessary thoughts and emotions. So, as you improve your attention, you also improve your emotional resilience.

- **Physical Resilience:** Whenever you train your attention, you force yourself and your body to remain still or focused on the task at hand. This improves your physical resilience because it makes you more in control of your physical motions.

Here are some ways to train your attention:

- **Break Tasks Into Manageable Chunks:** One of the easiest ways to train your attention is to break up tasks, work, or the day into manageable chunks. Many studies have shown that it is easier to focus your attention if it has a set time. At work, for example, set breaks every 52 minutes. If 52 minutes sounds like a lot for you, start with 20 minutes, and work your way up. This will train your psychological and physical resilience.

- **Be Mindful:** Another way to train your attention is to be mindful. Mindfulness is basically having a moment where you focus on the exact moment at hand, nothing before or after. An easy way to practice mindfulness is with a daily meditation, studies have shown that just 10 to 20 minutes of motivation today can improve your focus. Mindfulness improves all aspects of resilience.

- **Practice Attentive Listening:** Attentive listening is when you listen to another person without interrupting, recapping, or using connection words. It requires you to stay engaged in your listening abilities. Attentive listening trains all three forms of resilience.

- **Journaling At Night:** Another way to train your attention is to journal at night. Journaling at night will give you the chance to focus purely on your thoughts and feelings at that moment. Try to stay in the moment as closely as possible. If you make this into a habit, journaling will also turn into a healthy coping mechanism that will make you more psychologically and emotionally resilient.

By practicing some of these techniques every day, you will boost your mental dexterity and resilience even on days when things are going great.

CONCLUSION

As we have seen, resilience is an important part of life. If you are unable to bounce back from adverse situations, your life will feel difficult, meaningless, and unnecessarily disheartening. For this reason, it is imperative to train your resilience so that way you can bounce back and enjoy life to its fullest, no matter how difficult a situation may be.

In this book, we defined resilience as one's ability to bounce back from adverse situations, and looked at the four types of resilience, which includes psychological, emotional, physical, and community resilience. Additionally, we looked at the four main components of resilience, which includes connection, wellness, healthy thoughts, and meaning.

We then looked at how to develop these four components of resilience during difficult phases of life. More specifically, we looked at how to build connections during times of loss, how to foster wellness during times of poor mental and physical health, how to think healthy thoughts during difficult and uncontrollable times, and how to find purpose when you feel lost.

Finally, we looked at how to bring all four components together in order to practice resilience training. We specifically discussed how attention training can boost psychological, emotional, and physical resilience. More so, we recommend training your attention even on your good days so that you are ready for the bad ones.

Now that you have learned key strategies to boost your mental dexterity, you can bounce back from any situation and find yourself stronger than before. It is important to remember to be kind to and patient with yourself as you try to become more resilient. As we stated in chapter one, resilience is a journey, not a destination. The best way to enjoy your journey is to be kind and accept that change won't happen overnight.

You've got this!

RESILIENCE

CHECKLIST

CHECKLIST

- Defining resilience
    - Ability to bounce back
    - Come back stronger than before
    - Allows you to grow and heal
    - Overcome any adverse situation
- Why resilience is important
    - Improves your quality of life
    - Helps you find fulfillment
    - Helps you grow
    - Helps you face adverse situations
        - Changing careers
        - Work
        - Divorce
        - Death
        - Financial troubles
        - Moving
        - Raising children
    - When you aren't resilient
        - Feel overcome
        - Feel like you can't master adverse situations
        - Leads to burn out
- Factors of resilience
    - Social support
    - Realistic planning
    - Confidence
    - Healthy coping mechanisms
    - Strong communication
    - Regulating emotions

- Building resilience
  - You can build resilience
    - Resilience training
    - Anyone can benefit from resilience training
  - Resilience building is a journey
    - Not a destination
- Types of resilience
  - Psychological resilience
    - Thoughts
    - Reasoning
    - Problem-solving
  - Emotional resilience
    - Feelings
    - Emotions
  - Physical resilience
    - Physical capabilities
    - Body's ability to bounce back
  - Community resilience
    - Community's ability to bounce back during adverse times
      - Natural disasters
      - Terrorist attacks
      - School shootings
- Resilience helps
  - Major life problems
    - Death
    - Divorce
    - Getting fired
  - Temporary problems
    - Tough deadlines
    - Upcoming test
    - Minor fight with your spouse
  - Daily problems
    - Exercising
    - Daydreaming
    - Sleeping

- Components of resilience
  - Connection
    - Family
    - Friends
    - Coworkers
    - Community
  - Wellness
    - More than just your health
    - Physical wellness
    - Mental wellness
    - Emotional wellness
    - Personal growth
  - Healthy thinking
    - Thinking realistically, flexibly, and creatively
    - Accurate interpretation
    - Creative problem-solving
    - Recognizing thinking traps
  - Meaning
    - Connects events, ideas, and feelings into a greater purpose
    - Meaningfulness
    - Meaning gives context to resilience
- Connections during times of loss
  - Times of loss
    - Death
    - Divorce
    - Moving
    - Losing a job
  - Benefits of connections
    - Improves ability to cope
    - Alleviates effects of distress
    - Promotes lifelong good mental health
    - Improves self-esteem
    - Lowers cardiovascular risks
    - Promotes healthy lifestyle habits
  - Quality connections

- Quality over quantity
  - Quality
    - Cares for your wellbeing
    - Pushes you to grow
    - Supports you
  - Quantity
    - A lot of connections
    - Connections don't really care about you
    - Can't depend on any connections even though you have a lot
- How to build healthy connections
  - Put yourself out there
  - Volunteer
  - Join a fitness group
  - Take a class
  - Look online
- How to maintain healthy connections
  - Stay in touch
  - Don't get jealous
  - Listen
  - Give back
  - Don't overdo it
- Fostering wellness during times of poor mental and physical health
  - How to foster wellness for mental health
    - Start a gratitude journal
    - Meditate
    - Say positive affirmations
    - Talk to your connections
    - Talk to a health care professional
  - How to foster wellness for physical health
    - Exercise
    - Eat healthily
    - Get your friends involved
    - Sleep

- Thinking healthy thoughts during uncontrollable times
  - Uncontrollable times
    - Death
    - Getting fired
    - Natural disasters
    - Unforeseen life changes
    - Car accident
    - Health scares
  - How to think healthy thoughts
    - Recognize thinking traps
      - Overgeneralization
      - Black and white thinking
      - Labeling
      - Mind reading
      - Fortune telling
      - Mental filter
      - Emotional reasoning
      - "Should" statements
      - Discounting positives
    - Separate thoughts from actual events
    - Identify and challenge thinking traps
    - Accept limitations
- Finding purpose when you feel lost
  - Why purpose matters
    - Helps resilience have context
    - Provides motivation
    - Helps you see the big picture
    - Purpose creates meaning
  - How to find your purpose
    - Purpose involves three things
      - Something in the world you care about
      - What you love to do
      - Your natural talents

- Resilience training
    - Improves all aspects of resilience
        - Connections
        - Wellness
        - Thinking
        - Purpose
    - Helps you improve resilience
    - Improves resilience when you don't feel stressed
    - Teaches you good coping mechanisms
    - Types of resilience training
        - Training your attention
            - Improves psychological, emotional, and physical resilience
            - How to train attention
                - Break tasks into manageable chunks
                - Be mindful
                - Practice attentive listening
                - Journal at night

RESILIENCE

RESOURCE CHEAT SHEET

Defining Resilience

- What Is Resilience? Your Guide To Facing Life's Challenges, Adversities, and Crises, Everyday Health
- Building Your Resilience, American Psychological Association
- What Is Resilience? Psych Central
- What Is Resilience? Driven
- Resilience, Canter on the Developing Child Harvard University
- The Importance Of Resilience, Very Well Mind
- What Is Resilience And Why Is It Important To Bounce Back? Positive Psychology
- Resilience Skills, Factors And Strategies Of The Resilient Person, Positive Psychology
- Building Your Resilience, American Psychological Association
- Psychological And Social Aspects Of Resilience: A Synthesis Of Risks And Resources, U.S. National Library of Medicine National Institutes of Health

Types of Resilience

- Type Of Resilience, Open Pages
- The Four Types Of Resilience, Pallet One
- Other Types Of Resilience, Local Public Health Institute of Massachusetts
- Leading In A Crisis: 3 Kinds Of Resilience To Strive For, Government Technology
- Psychological Resilience, Science Direct
- What Is Psychological Resilience? YouTube, The Autiopedia
- Why Emotional Resilience Is A Trait You Can Develop, Very Well Mind
- What Is Emotional Resilience And How To Build It, Positive Psychology
- Why Is Physical Resilience Important? Martha Forlines
- Community Resilience, Public Health Emergency

Components of Resilience

- The 8 Key Elements Of Resilience, Psychology Today
- Five Components Of Resilience, Risk Views
- Four Key Components Of Resiliency, TRACOM
- The 6 Domains Of Resilience, Driven
- Cognitive And Behavioral Components Of Resilience To Stress, Science Direct
- Resilience Skills, Factors And Strategies Of The Resilient Person, Positive Psychology
- How To Measure Resilience With These 8 Resilience Scales, Positive Psychology
- Seven Elements Of Resilience, Central Coast ARAFMI

How to Build Connections

- Connections – The Key To Healing And Resilience, The New Social
- Four Ways Social Support Makes You More Resilient, Greater Good Magazine
- Connections, The Resilience Center
- Cultivating Connection And Resilience: When Your Team And Clients Are Apart, Association for Talent Developer
- Finding Connection And Resilience During the Corona Virus Pandemic, The New Yorker
- Connectedness: Relationships Strengthen Resilience, Nany Nav Stress
- The Best Ways to Build Meaningful Connections And Improve Relationships, Medium
- 10 Tips To Make New Friends, Personal Excellence
- 6 Ways To Become Closer With Your Family, Even As A Busy Adult, Bustle
- How To Get Connected In Your Community, Tree Hugger

How to Foster Wellness

- What Is Wellness? UC Davis
- What Is Wellness? Global Wellness Institute
- What Is Wellness And Why Is It Important? Total Access Medical
- Resilience And Wellness, Westchester Libraries
- Wellbeing And Resilience, Reach Out
- Building Resilience For Wellness, U.S. National Library of Medicine National Institutes of Health
- A Guide To Resilience And Wellbeing, The Resilience Institute
- Emotional Wellness Toolkit, National Institutes of Health
- 12 Ways To Foster Emotional Wellness, SC Thrive
- 5 Key Aspects Of Physical Wellness, RTOR

How to Think Healthy Thoughts

- Healthy Thinking: Building Emotional Resilience, Journey Well
- Building Resilience With The Power Of Positive Thinking, Practical Longevity
- Thinking Traps: 12 Cognitive Distortions That Are Hijacking Your Brain, Mindset Health
- Thinking Traps: How To Let Go Of Negative Thoughts, The Chelsea Psychology Clinic
- Negative Thinking Traps, Univeristy of Washington
- Stop Negative Thoughts: Choosing A Healthier Way Of Thinking, University Of Michigan Medicine
- Wellness Module 8: Healthy Thinking, Here To Help
- Benefits Of Thinking Positively, And How To Do It, Healthline
- 4 Ways To Think Yourself Healthy, Body + Soul

How To Find Purpose

- Building Your Resilience And Understanding Your Purpose, Smart Company
- How A Sense of Purpose Build Resilience In Teens, Newport Academy
- Purpose In Life Predicts Better Emotional Recover From Negative Stimuli, U.S. National Library of Medicine National Institutes of Health
- 4 Ways to Achieve Meaning And Purpose In Your Life, Psychology Today
- How To Find Your Purpose In Life, Greater Good Magazine
- 7 Tips For Finding Your Purpose In Life, Very Well Mind
- Five Steps To Finding Your Life Purpose, Psychology Today
- 3 Unexpected Ways To Find Your Life Purpose, HuffPost

Resilience Training

- Resilience Training, Mayo Clinic
- Building Resilience, Harvard Business Review
- Resilience Training: How To Master Mental Toughness And Thrive, Positive Psychology
- Attention Training For Learning Enhancement And Resilience, U.S. National Library of Medicine National Institutes of Health
- Mindfulness training In High Stress Professions: Strengthening Attention And Resilience, Science Direct
- Your Concentration Training Program: 11 Exercises That Will Strengthen Your, Attention, Art Of Manliness
- A Meditation To Focus Attention, Mindful

CPSIA information can be obtained
at www.ICGtesting.com
Printed in the USA
LVHW060443020221
678045LV00033B/1630